Always with Dignity

All rights reserved

Copyright Mike Devine 2011

ISBN 978-0-615-47660-5

Date of registration: April 11, 2011

To Domenica

For my family: Brigid, Bruce, Jamie, Marylin, Glenn, Christina, Cayden, Lauren, Daniele and Nancy;

and for my friends, especially Skip, Dr Jones, Robert, Agnes, Bobbi, Annie, Jeep, the Dubai design team and the Baldwin Park irregulars.

My gratitude to Jim Sanders, Claude Lambert and Skip Olsson.

Chapters

Introduction

1. There's no business like show business

2. Almost all creatures

3. To err is humam

4. Vive la France

5. This, That, the other Thing

6. Love is just around the corner

Introduction

For those of you who like words without pictures.

I have been lucky enough to be employed in the entertainment industry, working behind the scenes - actually creating the scenes - for more years than any sensible person should.
During those years, my mind has had the tendency to wander unchecked (unmoored might be more apt) and on the following pages are the results of some of the twisting trails that mind has taken for no rational reason. Certainly, recurring themes of Montana and sheep have no logical explanation, nor does a dose of French wordplay involving Vaseline - but here they are within the pages of this sketchbook awaiting the "Oh! Dear!" from friends and family as they nod knowingly and sadly shake their heads.

Be assured, though, the drawings are organic, eco-friendly and fat free; they are the result of years of wool gathering (sheep again) in darkened theaters, production meetings, team building meetings, airline lounges, freeway driving, hotel rooms and recreational drinking (seldom at the same time.)

I hope they bring a chortle or two and that the ink does not rub off on your fingers. Enjoy!

1. There's no business like show business

Audition!

"Actually, I'm in love with the balcony."

Pre - Comedy

"The Royal Shakespeare Company"

Basil - His moment!

The WAY Musketeers

Re-write!

"Lovely, Basil, but we're doing Lear ..."

Founder's night: Montana Symphony Orchestra

"Martyn, could I have a wee glance at the plans for the balcony scene?"

"He's too short."

The Incredible Sulk

Mime Control

Potato in Hollywood

Pepe the Wonderworm hears the worst from his agent......

"Certain segments have to go!"

-MW

Seth, the Wonderfish, overtrains

Nijinsky

The Bronx - Manhattan - Staten Island too!

Unsung Heroes

The bricklayer of Oz

Cirque du Bob

Imodium D !

Pinkey the Clown - R.I.P.

2. Almost all creatures...

Dreams of one last leap

"It was a low life dive in the dead end part of town....."

..it smelled like cheap booze
Stale cigarettes and lanolin"

The Amarillo Museum of Natural History

"So, who made him Harbinger?"

"Wait! Weren't we just penguins?"

"I hate his 'more endangered than thou' attitude"

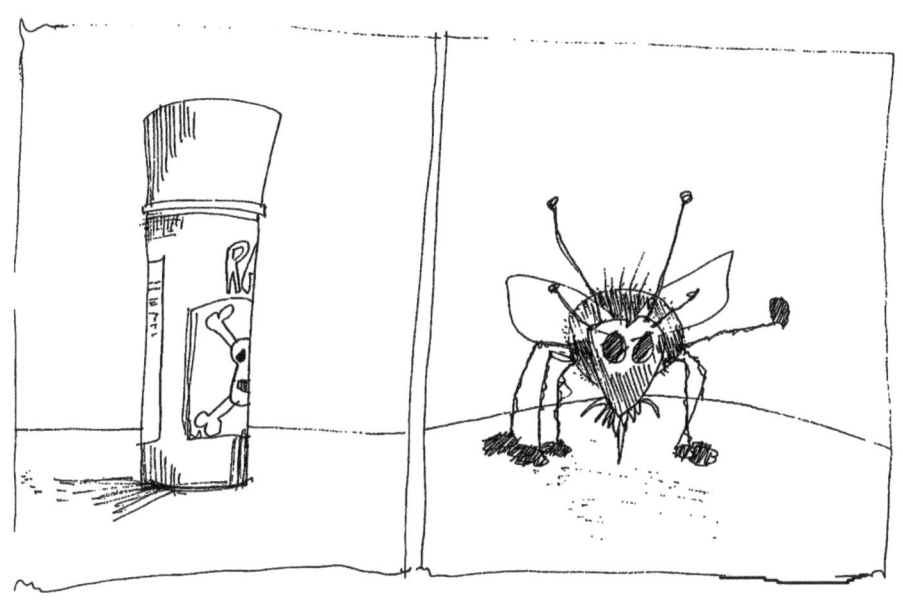

Insecticide   *Insectifront*

The Germinator

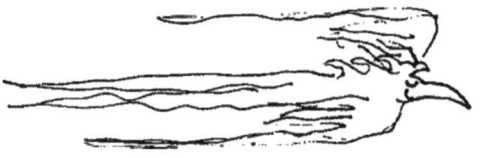

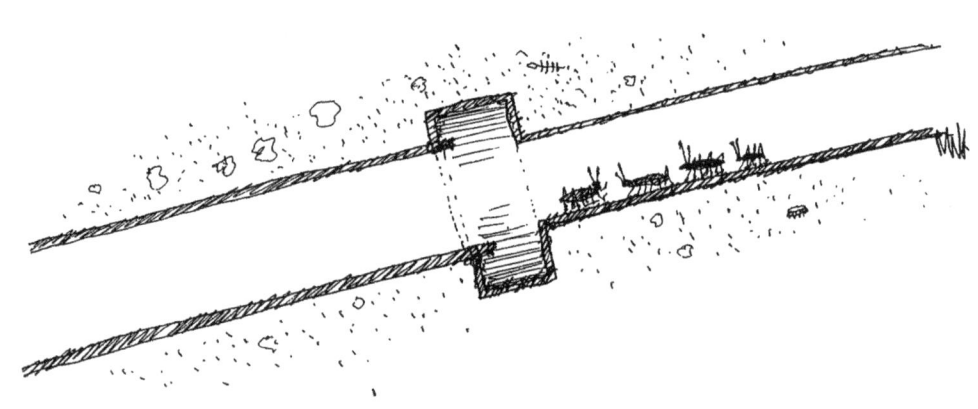

"Let's raise hell at the Ritz"

LONGSHOT

The lone prairie

The really lone prairie

The Royal Canadian Mounted Fleece

The shepherd tends his flock

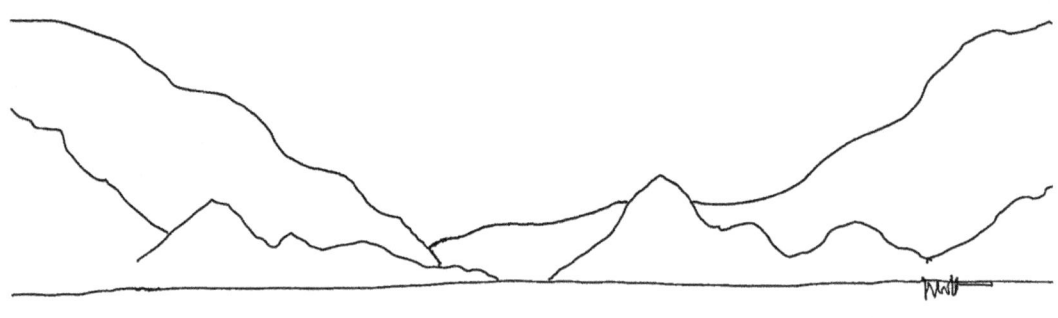

The Loch Ness Hamster

"Wow! Look at Skip's new hat!"

FAITH

HOPE

CHARITY

The Call of the Wild

"Does it make me look fat?"

Ménage à Montana

Cow trying to form a thought

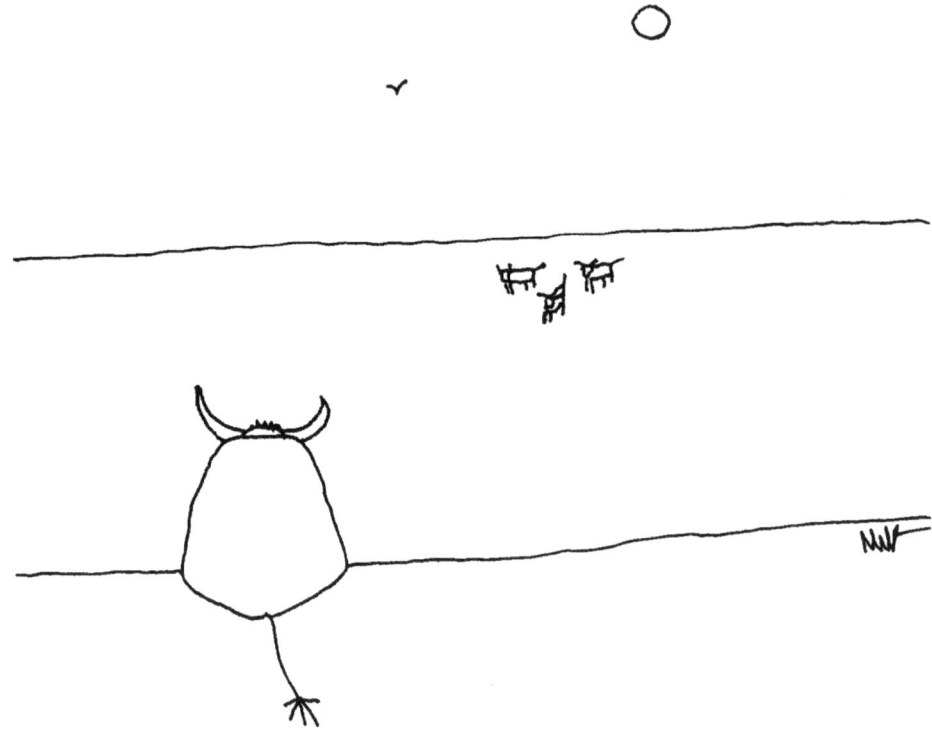

Sullen cow disease

3. To err is humam

Our entire genome

Sidney Jones and the Temple of Doom

"What if THIS is hell?"

"He says he's become a big picture guy"

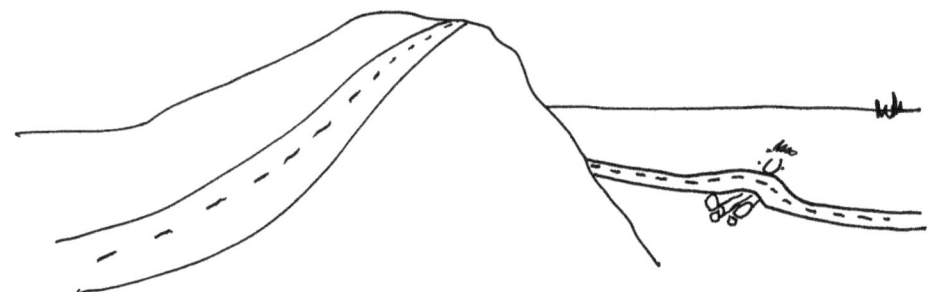

Over hill and Dale

Meanderthal

The Market

Miss Congeniality   *Miss Venality*

The Three Tenures

Aunt Farm

The WHAT - EVER Bowl

ART - imitating life

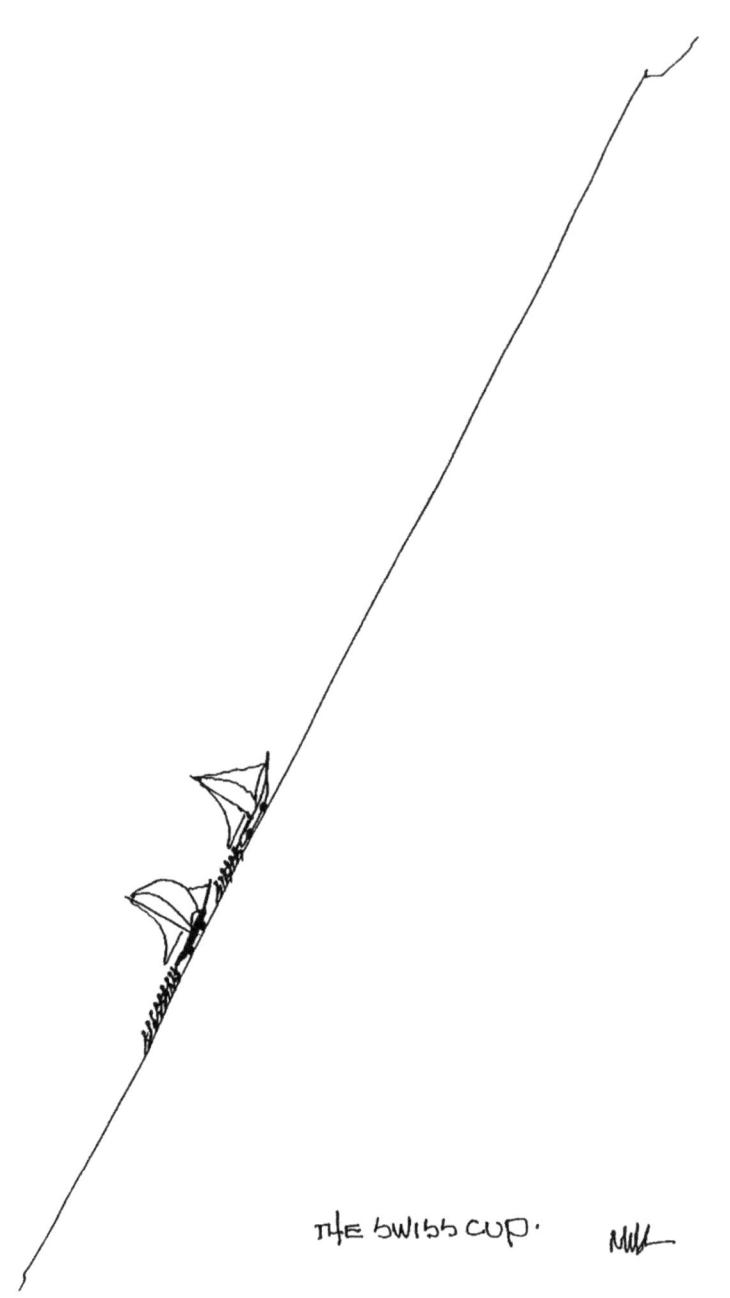

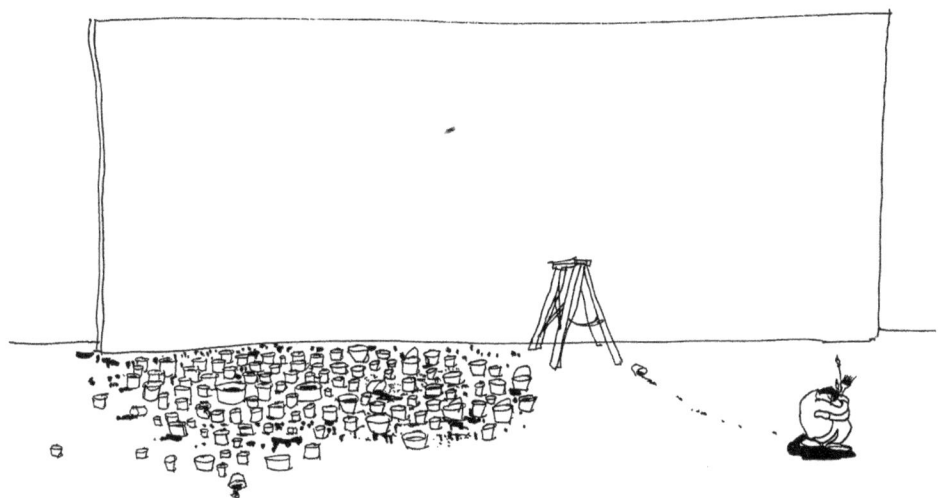

The artist begins (1)

The artist begins (2)

The Renaissance begins

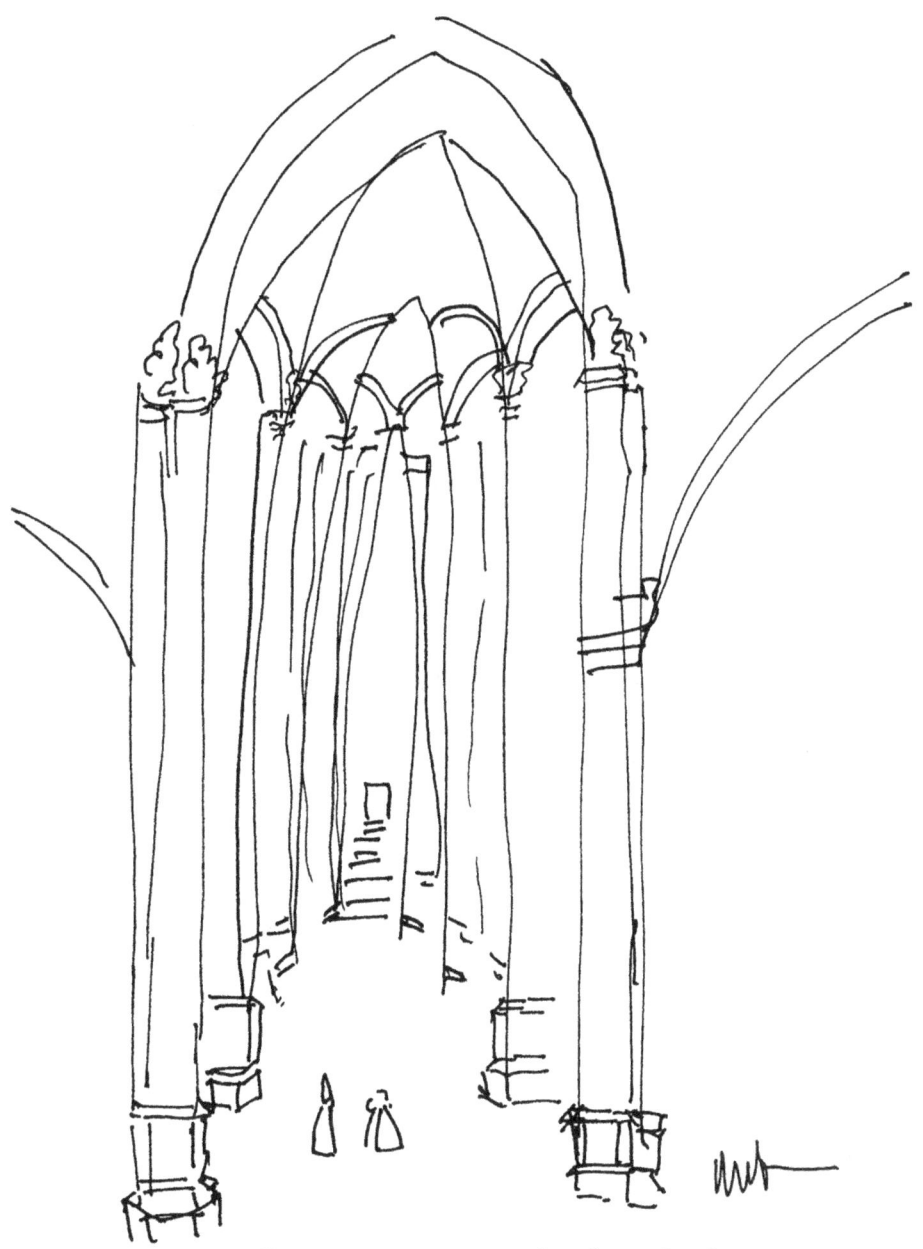

"*Let's jazz it up with a bit of color*"

·TOUR DE TRUMP·

"My body has turned to parody"

O'Malley is cleared for takeoff

Famous failures

Fulton's steam iron

Survivor - not the series

The news hour ends

4. Vive la France

Van, ordinaire

Grand Syrah

Petit Jeté

Laissez Fairy

"*Je me Vaseline*"

Les petits fours

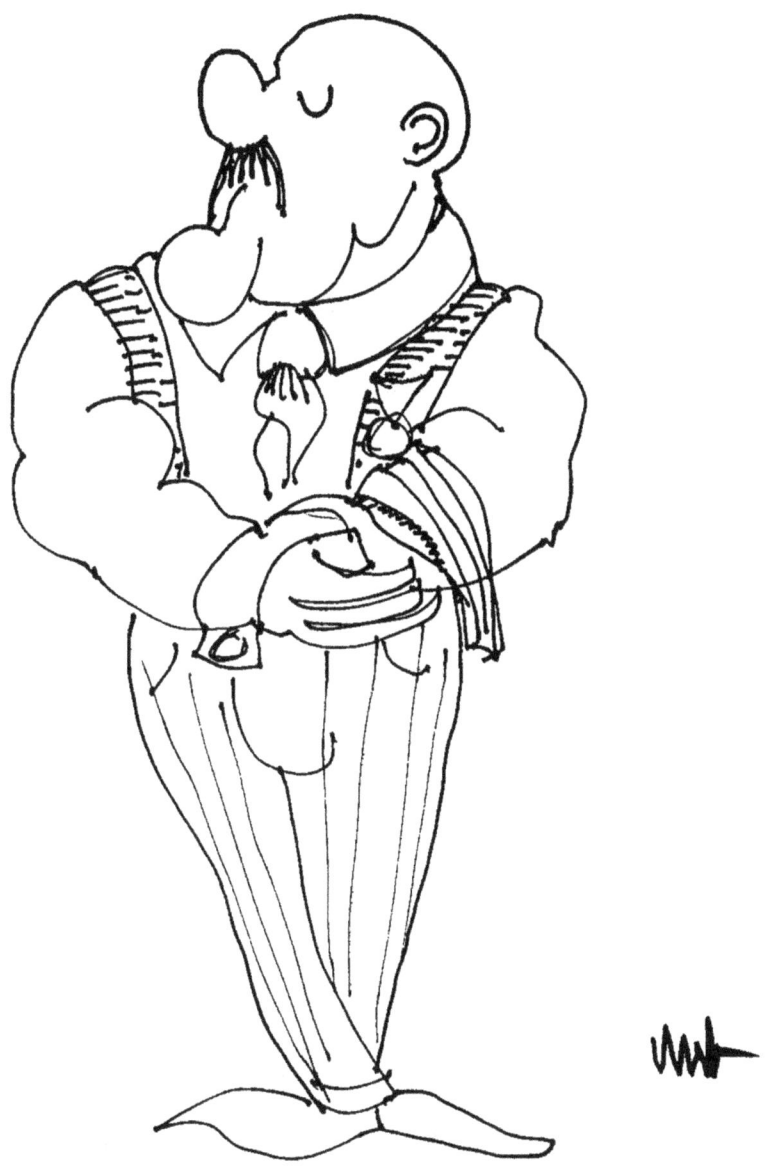

Le champ des Champs-Elysées

Brandy Alexander

CREPE SUZETTE.

Le Roué du Rivoli...

5. This, That, the other Thing

the other Thing

Spring!

Plein air

I AM _SO_ BORED!

Grant takes Richmond

The Niña, the Pinto and the Santa Maria

The Pony Local

To Bill Fremly, crop dusting was no laughing matter.

 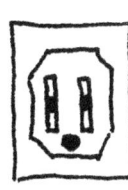

"Yes! But he's so grounded!"

The Final Four

Wrought iron   *Overwrought iron*

6. Love is just around the corner

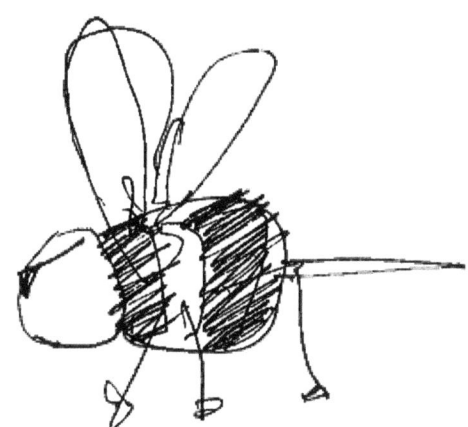

"Don't honey me!"

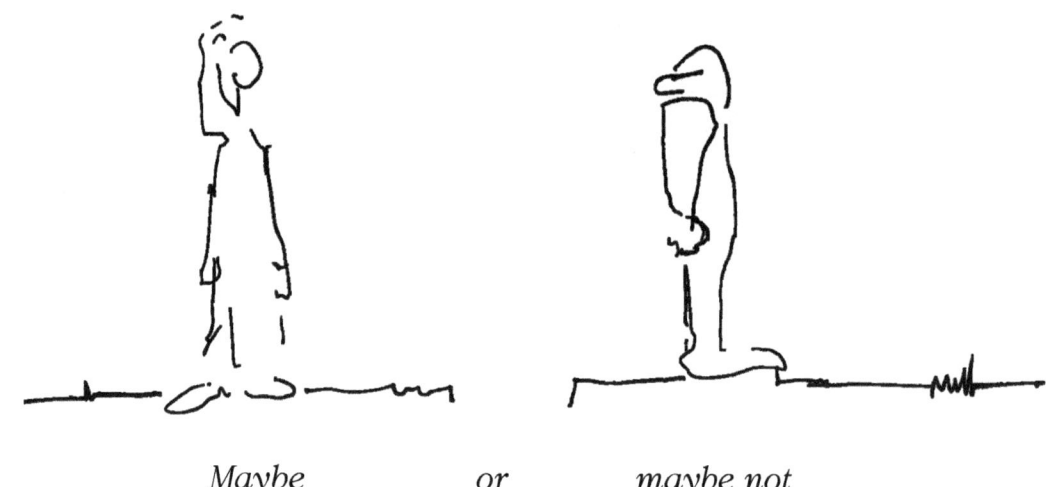

Maybe   or   maybe not

www.ingramcontent.com/pod-product-compliance
Lightning Source LLC
Chambersburg PA
CBHW081457040426
42446CB00016B/3277